Granny's Tree-climbing

TALKING CUB
Published by Speaking Tiger Books LLP
125A, Ground Floor, Shahpur Jat
New Delhi 110049

First published in paperback in Talking Cub by Speaking Tiger Books in 2022
Text copyright © Ruskin Bond 2022
Illustrations copyright © Ekta Bharti 2022

ISBN: 978-93-5447-302-9
eISBN: 978-93-5447-303-6

10 9 8 7 6 5 4 3 2 1

Printed at Millenium Offset Pvt Ltd.

No part of this publication may be reproduced, transmitted, or stored in
a retrieval system, in any form or by any means, electronic, mechanical,
photocopying, recording or otherwise, without the prior permission
of the publisher.

This book is sold subject to the condition that it shall not, by
way of trade or otherwise, be lent, resold, hired out, or otherwise circulated,
without the publisher's prior consent, in any form
of binding or cover other than that in which it is published.

Granny's Tree-climbing

Ruskin Bond

Illustrated by Ekta Bharti

talking CUB
An Imprint of Speaking Tiger Books

My grandmother was a genius. You'd like to know why?
Because she could climb trees. Spreading or high,
She'd be up their branches in a trice. And
            mind you,
When last she climbed a tree, she was sixty-two.
Ever since childhood, she'd had this gift
For being happier in a tree than in a lift;

And though, as years went by, she would be told
That climbing trees should stop when one
      grew old—
And that growing old should be gone
      about gracefully—
She'd laugh and say, 'Well, I'll grow
      old disgracefully.
I can do it better.' And we had to agree;

For in all the garden there wasn't a tree
She hadn't been up, at one time or another
(Having learned to climb from a loving brother
When she was six)—but it was feared by all
That one day she'd have a terrible fall.

The outcome was different—while we were in town
She climbed a tree and couldn't come down.
After the rescue,
The doctor took Granny's temperature and said,
'I strongly recommend a quiet week in bed.'
We sighed with relief and tucked her up well.

Poor Granny! For her, it was like a brief season in hell,
Confined to her bedroom, while every breeze
Whispered of summer and dancing leaves.
But she held her peace till she felt stronger,
Then sat up and said, 'I'll lie here no longer!'

And she called for my father and told him
    undaunted
That a house in a tree-top was what she
    now wanted.
My Dad knew his duties. He said, 'That's
    all right—
You'll have what you want, dear. I'll start
    work tonight.'

With my expert assistance, he soon finished
    the chore:
Made her a tree-house with windows and a door.

So Granny moved up, and now every day
I climb to her room with glasses and a tray.

RUSKIN BOND is the author of numerous novellas, short-story collections and non-fiction books, many of them classics. Among them are *When I Was a Boy, Lone Fox Dancing, The Room on the Roof, A Flight of Pigeons*, and *A Book of Simple Living*. He received the Sahitya Akademi Award in 1993, the Padma Shri in 1999 and the Padma Bhushan in 2014.

EKTA is a freelance illustrator who loves to draw animals, people, flowers and trees. She is most excited about collecting stories from here and there in her sketches, scribbles and colours. Often found smelling books, eating dark chocolate, speaking to dogs and basking in the sun, Ekta's most favourite hobby is to walk about hunting for sunlit grassy patches, investigating strange flowers and spotting hidden birds. She aspires to build a tiny house for herself and her cats someday in the middle of a thicket.